Teaching Your Child to Pray

TEACHING YOUR CHILD TO PRAY

Colleen Townsend Evans
Photographs by Walter Bredel

A Doubleday-Galilee Original

DOUBLEDAY & COMPANY, INC. GARDEN CITY, NEW YORK

With Mrs. Evans in the photographs are two young children,
Michelle Pitcher and Luke Dellavalle.

Some of the photos were taken at the Keokee Memorial Chapel (built
in 1838) in Paradise Valley, Pennsylvania.

Library of Congress Catalog Card Number 77-12847
ISBN 0-385-13249-2 Trade
0-385-14513-6 Prebound

FIRST EDITION

Preface

This book began as an idea in the mind of Randall E. Greene, Associate Editor at Doubleday, who thought it would be good if a book could bring parent and child together to talk about God and Jesus and prayer. He also thought that if the book could address both the parent and the child, it might serve as a starting point in a spiritual dialogue in which both might learn and grow. I certainly agreed.

Our four children are all now in college or graduate school. However, I remember well when they were as young as the lively children who posed with me for the pictures in this book—that inquisitive period, which seems to begin at a very early age indeed. There were so many questions!—"Who is God?" "Where is God?" "Can I talk to Jesus?" "How can I pray?" I know it was a time when Louis and I learned at least as much as our children did. Such moments are some of the most precious in family life.

And so that is why this book takes on a special format. The text set in regular type addresses the parent, and the large type addresses the child—although we hope each will explore the other's side of the page. It is not a book of questions and answers, nor does it assume that the parent is the teacher and the child the student. Far from it! In the eyes of God, we all are children, and Jesus is our teacher. If anything, the parent has more to learn from the child, because one of the first things Jesus teaches us is that, in order to understand the things of God, we must become childlike. If we can do that, then when he holds out his hand, we will grasp it in complete trust. Where he leads us, we will follow, not as a somber duty but as a joyful adventure.

So, here we sit, parent and child, at the Master's feet. And we ask him—much as the disciples did—"Lord, teach us to pray."

I want to thank Randy Greene for his good idea—Laura Hobe for her editorial assistance—Walter Bredel for his sensitive photography—Diana Klemin for artistic direction—and my friends Linda LeSourd and Renee Liebner for bouncing ideas back and forth with me. I am also indebted to the Bible scholars who have shared their thoughts in print with us—to my husband, Louis Evans, Jr., who always stimulates my mind and throws new light on whatever path I am following—and to our children, who bless me with their friendship and enthusiastic support.

COLLEEN TOWNSEND EVANS
Washington, D.C.

Teaching Your Child to Pray

THE LORD'S PRAYER

Our Father who art in heaven,
Hallowed be thy name. Thy kingdom come.
Thy will be done on earth, as it is in heaven.
Give us this day our daily bread.
And forgive us our debts,
as we forgive our debtors.
And lead us not into temptation,
but deliver us from evil:
For thine is the kingdom, and the power,
and the glory . . . forever. Amen.

MATTHEW 6: 9b-13

We can talk with God, you know. Even though we can't see him, he is always very close to us—close to you, and close to me, and close to every person in the world.

When we talk with God, and God talks with us, we call it praying. And what we say to God is called a prayer.

Praying is easy to do. You can fold your hands if you want to. You can bow your head if you want to. You can whisper, or talk out loud, or you can talk without making a sound. But you don't have to do any of these things—unless you want to—because praying is a little different for each of us.

The important thing is to go right ahead and talk to God now— just as you would to the most special friend you've ever had.

Prayer is a way of getting close to God. As we push aside distractions and focus our thoughts on God, we make a clearing for our spirit to reach out and touch God. No need to wonder whether we will find him, for he is always there.

For some of us, praying is difficult. Where do we begin? Should we use special words—words we never use when we talk to anyone else? Are we supposed to pray in a certain tone of voice? Or fold our hands, or sit, or kneel?

Any one of these things—even all of them—may help us to pray, but none of them is necessary. Worrying about them can even hinder our praying, for they aren't what prayer is about. Prayer is communication, and whatever helps us to communicate with the Lord we love and are loved by—*that's* important. And, as in any good relationship, communication has to go both ways.

We don't have to be formal, for God is not an occasional visitor. If we have accepted his Son, Jesus Christ, into our hearts, then God makes his home in our lives.

There are no right words to say, no proper way to speak, no correct positions to take. There is only our awareness of God's presence, our trust in his guidance for every moment of our lives, our willingness to put ourselves—body, mind, and spirit—in his hands.

How do we begin? Simply: by talking to God as we would to a friend we love and trust completely.

There are lots of ways you can pray.

When you wake up in the morning, you can say "Good morning" to God and ask him to be very close to you all day.

You can pray on your way to school and ask him to help you understand all the things you are going to learn.

You can pray when you're with your friends, and ask God to help you be a good friend.

You can pray with your family when you sit down to eat, and thank God for the food he has given you.

You can pray before you go to sleep at night. You can ask God to take care of your mother and father and sisters and brothers, and all the people you know and love. You can ask God to be with everybody, everywhere.

Yes, you can ask God to take care of you, too.

There are so many ways and so many times to pray, because praying doesn't mean that we interrupt life. It's part of life. In fact, prayer keeps us going in the midst of our daily struggles, our ups and downs. Jesus knew that—for he couldn't live without this direct, personal contact with his Father. And neither can we.

When Paul tells us to "Pray without ceasing" (I Thessalonians 5:17), he doesn't mean that every time we talk to God we shut everything else out. He was very much aware that we have other needs, other responsibilities, and other relationships in our lives.

But if, when we awake in the morning, we are aware of God, that is a form of praying. If, as we do our work and interact with others, we can turn to God for help at the very moment we feel the need for it, then that, too, is a genuine way of praying. If we are sensitive to the nudgings of the Holy Spirit and depend on him to help us choose our direction, that is another way we can pray. The key is the attitude of our hearts, for that is what God hears. He hears beyond our words to what we truly feel and mean.

So when you really think about it, we don't ever have to be without prayer, not even for a moment.

Prayer isn't just a lot of words.

Prayer means telling God how you think and how you feel, even if your thoughts and feelings aren't always good. God wants us to tell the truth. He understands. He doesn't want us to make believe we're happy if we really aren't happy.

So, if you're angry, then tell God that you're angry. And if you don't feel like praying, tell God you don't feel like praying and ask him to help you. He will. Just remember, always tell him the truth.

The important thing is to be *honest* with God. If we merely mouth some words of prayer while we're thinking about something else, then God can't possible hear us—because we aren't really praying. We might as well be reciting a nursery rhyme or reading names at random from a telephone book.

Real prayer involves an act of will. We have to bring our minds and our hearts into whatever it is we want to say to God—or we are saying nothing at all. So let's get honest with ourselves and honest with God. If we feel it, let's say it. If we don't feel it, let's not say we do.

Everybody gets angry at times, and when we're all stirred up, it's pretty hard to pray—unless we are able to pray honestly, pouring out our hearts before our God. Unless we are able to say, "Lord, I'm angry. You know it. I know it. Is it okay to feel this way? I mean, would the cause of my anger also anger you? Or am I all wound up in myself, acting on my own, instead of letting you guide my feelings?"

Sometimes we just aren't in the mood to pray. We may be depressed, we may be preoccupied, or we may not feel that "glow" we like to feel when we are in God's presence. Well, as someone very wise said, "When you cannot pray as you would, pray as you can."

You can always tell God exactly how you feel. You can always say, "Lord, I don't feel like praying, but here I am anyway. Help me." That's a prayer. Honestly.

We can pray when we're with other people. But it's good to pray all by ourselves sometimes. Then we don't have anything or anybody else to think about. Just God.

If you want to be all by yourself with God, you can go in your room and close the door and pray. But you don't have to have your own room. Lots of us don't. You can go outside and pray. Or you can stay right where you are and not think about anything or anybody else, except God. Because God is your friend. And it's good to be with your friend.

Wherever we are, whatever we may be doing—even when surrounded by other people—we can pray, and God will hear us. Praying "on the run" is so easy, so convenient, and it's the way we pray most of the time.

But praying is more than being heard. It is a relationship with someone we love, and if that love is to deepen, then we and the one we love must spend time together—time alone, without distractions, interruptions, or even the good company of friends and family.

Jesus said, "When you pray, enter into your inner chamber, and having shut your door, pray to your Father who is in secret" (Matthew 6:6). Well, not many of us have such a room, and neither did most of the men and women who listened to Jesus speak those words. There are people in our world who will live and die with-

out ever having privacy, and yet they, and all of us, can still spend time alone with God—because the key word here is "inner." Quite possibly, when Jesus spoke of an *"inner* chamber," he meant not a room in the literal sense but a place within ourselves, a quiet portion of our consciousness reserved for conversations with our Lord. This is a room available to rich and poor alike.

Perhaps we will find it difficult to go into our room regularly, or to stay as long as we would like. The important thing is for us to set aside such a room and not stay away from it too long. It is here that our spirit receives nourishment.

It may be inconvenient to pray this way. It certainly *is* difficult. But if we are going to be influenced by God, then we must seek out his company.

Sometimes, when we pray, God wants to talk to us. So we shouldn't do all the talking. Part of the time we should be very quiet and listen, and give God a chance to say something.

But God probably won't speak in words, the way you do. He might give you a feeling that you should do something—or that you shouldn't do something. He might make you think about someone or something you didn't expect to think about. He might give you a good idea. He might even help you understand something you didn't understand before.

Some of us say, "I never hear God—he doesn't speak to me." But do we give him a chance? Or do we barge into his presence and talk, talk, talk, without giving him a chance to speak? There cannot possibly be a friendship between two people when one of them does all the talking.

Listening is part of praying, perhaps the most important part. It is during these times of quiet that God can bring ideas into our minds, awaken concerns in our hearts, and even help us untangle a daily routine.

If we listen for God to speak in a big, resounding voice and in specific words, then we may miss his message. Sometimes God's voice is loud and the words clear—but more often we will be conscious of a gentle stillness, something like the "still small voice" heard by the prophet Elijah after the roar of wind, earthquake, and fire (I Kings 19:11–13). And suddenly we will know which way we are to walk, or what we are to do. Perhaps we will sense a direction or come to a decision that is totally unexpected, something we weren't even thinking about. Perhaps we will understand something that had been absolutely mystifying—until now, until we stopped talking, relaxed, and listened with our soul.

THE LORD'S PRAYER 凡凡

Now you are ready to pray a very beautiful and very important prayer called "the Lord's Prayer." This is a prayer that Jesus prayed to God, his Father, and he taught us how to pray it too.

Each word has a special meaning.

We can pray it together. Are you ready?

Let's begin. . . .

An exasperated young man once moaned, "Everybody tells me to pray, but nobody tells me *how!*"

The disciples of Christ must have felt the same way. They often saw Jesus praying and must have yearned for such a personal communion with God. Finally one of them said to Jesus, "Lord, teach us to pray." The disciple wasn't asking for words to memorize. He probably understood that praying meant talking to God from the depths of the heart. But now he was asking, "What is a prayer?"—or rather, "What shall we talk to God about?" *How* should we pray?

Characteristically, Jesus explained by doing—by praying what we know as "the Lord's Prayer." In these most beautiful and simple words, he tells us that there are six basic topics of conversation when one is talking to God. And, amazingly, they seem to cover just about everything that might be on the minds or in the hearts of men and women—and that which is important to God himself.

As the New Testament scholar William Barclay said, "In the Lord's Prayer, Jesus teaches us to bring the whole of God to the whole of life."

Our 父父

We don't say "my" Father or "your" Father, because God isn't just my Father or your Father. God is everyone's Father. He has children all over the world, and they are our brothers and sisters.

God loves all his children very much, so when we say "our" Father, we must think about all our other brothers and sisters and ask to love them the way God loves them. But there will be times when you won't like some of your brothers and sisters. And even times when some of them won't like you. When that happens, you can ask God to show you what he loves about them, and that will help you love them, too.

Because if God loves them—and he does—that makes them special.

When we pray, it is important to understand what our relationship with God is, and the very first word of the Lord's Prayer tells us where we stand. This is not an I-me-my prayer, and you will not find those pronouns in it. This is a we-us-our prayer, a family prayer for the children of God. And once we yield our lives to God, we become members of that family. We will have our spats and our sibling rivalries—that's perfectly healthy. But we cannot claim God as our Father and refuse to accept his other children, all of whom he loves as deeply as he loves us. We cannot pray this prayer without an awareness of our relatedness to others.

Think of the pain felt by an earthly mother and father whose children reject each other. Then imagine the pain we inflict upon God when we reject our brothers and sisters for any reason—education, cultural background, race, personal preference, a different opinion, or a personality quirk.

And since God does love each of us, then we have an additional responsibility to accept ourselves. So many of us suffer the worst kind of maladies, both physical and emotional, because we feel unworthy of anyone's love and we reject ourselves. But if God is *our* Father, then each of us is of great worth, and we cannot possibly be unloved—ever.

Our ℛ ℛ

And because God loves you, you are special, too.

Father 🗲 🗲

When you pray to God, you can tell him everything, and he will understand. He is the one who created you, and that is why you can call him "Father." He is your Father, your parents' Father, and everyone's Father.

Even though God has such a big family, he cares about you and me and each one of his children. He wants to know all about you— what you think, how you feel, if you're happy or sad. When you need any kind of help, you can go to him. Just tell him what's wrong, and he will know what to do.

But don't go to him only when you want some *thing*. Go to him sometimes when all you want is to be *with* him.

It is hard for us to understand how startled the disciples may have been when Christ told them to address God as their Father. Almighty God, Creator of heaven and earth and of man himself, Father of the national Israel—yes. But an almost-earthly parent, a Father to whom one can come for guidance, help, comfort, and even the bare necessities of life? "Indeed," Jesus was saying, "this is one of the things I came to tell you. You are God's children . . . both as a people and as individuals."

Sometimes we have the same problem. Even though we are accustomed to saying "Our Father," we don't always realize what the words mean. God—to many of us—is someone far away, majestic, almost aloof. Powerful, but not quite approachable, and certainly not interested in the daily goings-on in our humdrum lives. But what a mistake it is to think of God in those terms! He *is* our Father—a perfect Father, exceeding even the best earthly fathers. He has created the very life our existence celebrates. We are not robots programmed to move about, performing predetermined tasks until our parts wear out. We are human beings, members of mankind, and it is God who has given us the miracle of life that brought us into existence. He has also given us the earth to shelter and nourish us.

God is the original Father, the pattern for all earthly fathers to follow. This is what Paul might have meant when he said, "I bow my knee to the Father from whom every family in heaven and earth is named" (Ephesians 3:14–15).

Father

If you ask God to be close to you all the time, he will be there.

How do you feel when your mother or father isn't home? They aren't right there where you can see them, are they? But you know they love you. You know they are still your parents, and you are never beyond their love and care.

Well, God is like that. He loves and wants to be with you all the time. Maybe you can't see him, but he is there in your heart. And he will never go away.

An almost-earthly Father, yes—but God is also our Father in another sense, if we choose to let him be.

A flesh-and-blood child can have only a limited relationship with a Father who is spirit. Such a child cannot even master the language of such a parent. But God, in his original design for us, created another dimension of life, one that was spirit, one that was so sensitive to the thoughts and feelings of God that language was no barrier. This creature would be God's close friend and would never die. Eventually it would leave the earth and go to be with God, to continue forever the marvelous relationship that had grown up between them.

It was such a beautiful plan. And so simple! It would begin with the flesh-and-blood child, then at a later time—a time uniquely right for each individual—there would be another birth, a birth of the spirit within that child. In that way God would become Father in a very personal way. And the spirit would live and grow within the child, making possible the most intimate, loving relationship with the child's Parent. For the human child, it means having the spirit of God right there within him for all of his life—and even forever.

Life itself has been given outright to the human child by human parents. This second birth is different. There is a choice. The child can have it if the child wants it, if the child longs for the presence of its Father as the Father longs for the child. It is a gift to be claimed by a loving child from a loving Father. The child needs only to reach out and receive.

who art in heaven ௨ ௨

When you pray, you don't have to look up at the sky, because that isn't the only place where God is. You can look anywhere— up, down, over your shoulder, or anywhere. You can look at the trees, or at a building. You can look at flowers, or birds, or animals. You can look at your friends or your family. You can even close your eyes. Because God is in all these places.

God is everywhere and God is in everything good. He is in our heads, where we think, and in our hearts, where we feel. Whenever we do something nice for somebody, God knows it. Whenever we don't like somebody or hurt somebody, God knows that, too. And no matter where we are, God can find us and love us—because God is everywhere.

So often, when we pray, we look up at the sky, as if there were a certain portion of it we could designate as the dwelling place of God. Heaven, we seem to think, is "up there" somewhere.

Well, it isn't. Heaven *is* the dwelling place of God, but you won't find it in a fixed location. It is up there, down here, inside ourselves, and in every part of creation—because everywhere God is, is heaven. And since God is a spirit, he can be everywhere at one and the same time. He can share the most personal moments of our lives and still be Lord of the universe.

We can approach our Heavenly Father freely, but not carelessly. Much as he loves us, he is not an easygoing "Pop" who will wink at the way we hurt each other. He is not blind to our sins, nor can we hide them from him. For he is here, and there—and everywhere. There is nothing he does not see or hear or know. And there is no corner in all the world, or in the hearts of any of us, where his love and power cannot reach.

⚘ Hallowed be thy name

This phrase is so simple, yet once we understand its deeper meaning, it can change our lives.

Here we are, ready to pray, our hands filled with our needs and requests—and Jesus tells us to put all that aside. The first three requests in the Lord's Prayer belong to God.

And so we begin by praying that we, God's created children, will be able to fulfill our Heavenly Father's desires—and the first one has to do with the hallowing of his name.

Perhaps we have been saying this word "hallowed" since we were children, repeating it along with other words and phrases we learned by heart. Now it is time to find out what this word really means.

There must be many things you want to say to God. There must be many things you need.

But wait—Before you ask God for something, God wants to ask you for something.

That's right. Now it is time for you to give something to God, something he wants very much. We call it "hallowing his name."

But the word "hallowing" is hard to understand. So, first, let's find out what it means.

Hallowed be thy name ✗ ✗

Hallowing God's name means making God the most important one in our lives. It means that his name is very special to us.

Hallowing God's name means that God comes first. It means we want to honor—or please—God in all we do, or say, or think.

We ask God to help us live this way. We do it when we pray.

And, remember, we can put God first—anytime, anywhere, no matter what we're doing.

Since we don't ordinarily use the word "hallowed" these days, we have to go back in time to gain some insight into it.

To the ancient Greek, "hallowed" meant something unique and separate from other things. And to the ancient Hebrew, a name was more than a label: it was the personality, character, and nature of a person—his essence. So when we pray, "Hallowed be thy name," we are really saying, "O Lord, we want to be reverent, and we choose to give you the unique place in our lives which your loving, holy nature deserves."

That place is at the very center of our being—and that is how our lives are changed. The smallest, most unimportant thing we do becomes special when we do it as unto the Lord. For we begin to live our lives not as we would choose but as God would have us live—in word, deed, thought, and even in attitude. This is what is known as honoring God. It is what the Westminster Shorter Catechism means when it states, "Man's chief aim is to glorify God and to enjoy him forever."

But now—how do we go about that? In practical terms?

Hallowed be thy name

Hallowing God's name means that we think about other people, and not only about ourselves.

We think about people who are hungry, and we ask God what we can do to give them food. We think about people who are all alone, and we ask God to help us be their friends. We think about people who are old, and we ask God to help us remember to talk to them, and to care for them more.

We think about people who don't like each other just because they are different from each other, and we ask God to help us remember that each one of us is different because God made us that way. And being different is good.

We think about the earth where we live and we ask God to show us how to take good care of it.

When we do all these things—and more—we are hallowing God's name.

Prayer can give you peace of heart so you can sleep at night. But prayer can also make you so aware of the world's needs that you cannot sleep.

We honor God by being willing to get up off our knees and go into action about the things that concern him. We are not trying to earn our way to his love, because Christ has already shown us the way to his love. But now we are part of God's creation and he has work for us to do. His children have needs: the sick are lonely, the poor are hungry and unsheltered, the aged are neglected, the races oppress each other, the earth itself is being ravaged. If God is at the center of our lives—if we are truly hallowing his name—then his concerns become our concerns and we have to do something about them.

Thy kingdom come

We pray, "Thy kingdom come," because it means we want God to send his Son, Jesus, back to earth to be with us again. We don't know when that will happen, but when it does, it will be wonderful! No one will lie or cheat or steal. Everyone will love everyone else. No one will be lonely or sad. We won't have to be afraid of anything. And no one will die, or even get sick.

But in the meantime . . .

We are not easily impressed these days. Royalty does not dazzle us, political power is here one day and gone the next, and we simply don't believe promises of "pie in the sky."

But Jesus said, "My kingdom is not of this world," and that is different. This kingdom is not a place designed by man. It is a way of life originated by God himself. According to Paul, "The kingdom of God . . . means righteousness and peace and joy in the Holy Spirit" (Romans 14:17), and it is hard to imagine anything more wonderful than that.

The Bible tells us that someday Jesus will return to earth, bringing this kingdom with him—a time many Christians long for. And no wonder! We all dream of a better world, a world free of imperfections. We are tired of cheating and lying, sickness, death, and decay. We want no more of hatred and fear. We are homesick for God and his kingdom. And it is quite right for us to feel this way, for we must not lose sight of this dream.

But in one sense it isn't right—not if dreaming makes us lazy Christians who sit back and let God do all the work. There is much to be done, and in obedience to our Lord we should be about the task of building the kingdom of God.

K K K

We can make the world more like the world God wants it to be if we try to do the kind of things Jesus would do if he were here right now.

That means we must ask God to help us remember to tell the truth, and to try not to hurt anyone out of spite, ever. It means we must ask God to remind us to visit our friends when they are lonely or sick. It means we must ask God to help us treat all people kindly, and to keep us from getting angry when we don't have any good reason to be angry. It means that we must ask God to help us be the person he wants us to be so that our world can be more like the world he wants it to be.

When we allow Christ to become the center of our lives, we are saying, "Thy kingdom come, Lord—now—to me. I choose to go your way. Let your kingdom come in my life. Let me make a difference in the world." *K K*

Thy will be done 🜲 🜲

Another thing God likes is for us to pay attention to what he wants us to do. And then he wants us to go ahead and do it. That is what we mean by "doing God's will."

Sometimes we don't want to do these things. Sometimes we want to do something else. But God knows what is best for us, and he never asks us to do anything that isn't good for us—because he loves us and wants us to be happy.

So in our prayers it is best not to be always telling God what we want to do. Instead, some of the time we must listen and let God tell us what *he* wants us to do.

God has the best ideas of all. He's much wiser than we are!

Some of the most startling photographs ever taken are the pictures of the earth taken from space. What a beautiful jewel this planet is, its blues and browns and greens and whites so exquisitely arranged. And yet the earth is not just a bauble decorating the universe. It is a world of potential loveliness and health and goodness created by God and placed in our hands—not to do with as we please, but to do with as God wills.

We have a lot of good ideas—and a lot of bad ones. We don't follow through very well, and we make a lot of mistakes. So it isn't a good idea for us to insist on having our own way, or to think of prayer as a means of

coercing God. He loves us and wants us to be happy, but he knows far better than we do what is best for us.

That's why, when we pray, instead of trying to coax God around to our point of view, we want to align our wills with God's. That may take time. It won't always be easy—it certainly wasn't for Jesus in Gethsemane. But if the kingdom of God already exists within us, then we have help from the inside. As we are flexible and yielded to God, he will reveal to us his way, which is always best. And, what is more, he will give us joy in the doing. *R R*

As as on earth,
as it is in heaven

In heaven, everyone does God's will, and everyone likes to do it. And God wants us to do his will here on earth, too, as it is done in heaven.

Is there something God wants you to do for someone? Why don't you ask him—now!

This is not a casual request we are making. In fact, it can be costly. For in heaven, Jesus tells us, God's name is hallowed, his kingship already exists. His power is ultimate and his will is done—not with resignation, but with joy. Here on earth it is supposed to be the same—at least, that is what we are praying will happen.

Let's take a look at our earth as we know it.

Can anyone believe it is God's will for people to hate one another? To slaughter one another? For white and black to oppress one another? Can anyone believe it is God's will for children to be neglected and abused? For one third of the world to starve while the rest of us eat too much? There is no end to the things we see that tell us God's will is *not* being done fully here on earth. Yet all of them are things *we* can do something about. We, as people, cause the problems; as people, we can become part of the solutions.

Doing good is not something to postpone until we get to heaven. God wants his will done here on earth, too. He wants us to be his agents, his hands and feet. We can't do it all by ourselves, and he doesn't expect us to. He will supply the power if we will supply the willingness. We need not be concerned with our ability as much as with our avail-ability. If we will leave our hearts open to him, he will give us the compassion to sense the need wherever it is.

But the only way to pray honestly "Thy will be done on earth as it is in heaven" is to get involved in that will . . . to be open to respond as God moves us.

Thy kingdom come
Thy will be done
on earth, as it is in heaven

Let's put together all the things God wants from us:

First, he wants to be the most important one in our lives. Second, he wants us to listen when he tells us to do something. Third, he wants us to do what he tells us to do—and he wants us to enjoy doing it.

Don't forget—start your prayer by praying this way. Ask God to help you give him what he wants, and should have.

Now it all comes together.

The kingdom of God is both here and there. The kingdom of God is a community of God's children here on earth, a community of human beings who strive to do things the way God wants them done—as they are done in heaven. And any place where the will of God is done, *is* his kingdom.

These, then, are the requests that belong to God.

Give us this day our daily bread ⚡ ⚡

Now it is time to ask for the things we need. That doesn't mean we can have anything we please—because God knows that wouldn't be good for us. It would make us selfish and greedy.

When you ask for something, ask God if he thinks you ought to have it. He'll know, and if it is something good and right for you, then he will give it to you.

We would have asked for what *we* wanted, but now we want what God wants *for us*. We are conscious of a different purpose in our lives because God is at the center of ourselves. We are not simply here; we are here to do his work and honor his name. What we need are the tools to do that work.

The next three petitions are ours. Now it is time to share with God what we feel to be our need, and ask him to give it to us—if he agrees that we need it. That last clause is very important, for if we had begun this prayer by thinking about ourselves instead of about God, our personal requests would have been very different.

Give us this day our daily bread ⚡

The world "bread" means something we need, not just
something we want. If we see something and want to have it,
and yet we're not at all sure what we'll do with it, that's a sign
that we really don't need it. But if we see something and want it
because we can do something good with it, then we really need
it.

So before you ask God for something, think about what you
want to do with it once you have it.

Bread—surely it isn't simply part of a loaf.

Some scholars believe that the word "bread" in this prayer means Christ himself, since Jesus calls himself "the bread of life" (John 6:33–35). That would mean we are asking God for spiritual nourishment, which, of course, we are. But Jesus has told us to ask God for everything we need.

Some people feel uncomfortable praying for anything material or physical or even intellectual. They think God cares only about our spirits and couldn't care less about the basic realities of life, such as money to pay our bills, a roof over our heads, food for our bodies, and solutions to our problems. Well, when any teaching is so spiritualized that it belittles our bodies and minds, it also belittles the creation God called good! God made our bodies and minds as well as our spirits, and he cares very much about each part of the whole person.

Of course, it's disastrous to be preoccupied with wealth or material things or getting ahead or even with our own thoughts. But it's also disastrous when necessity forces us to be preoccupied with what we *don't* have and really need. God has better things for us to do with our time and energies. He wants us to bring all our needs to him and trust him to answer them in the way that is best for us. Then we can be free to go out and work for him—with the resources we need to do the task.

𝕽 𝕽 Give us this day our daily bread

But don't be shy—ask God for whatever you need. He wants you to tell him these things because he is your Father and he loves you.

If you are hungry, if you are sick, if you are sad, if you have lost something, if your friend won't talk to you, if you are having trouble in school—or anything—you can ask God to give you what you need.

Ask God for what you want and what you need, but tell him, too, that if he has something different in mind, you'll take that instead.

Martin Luther said that daily bread "includes everything needed for this life, such as food and clothing, home and property, work and income, a devoted family, an orderly community, good government, favorable weather, peace and health, a good name, and true friends and neighbors" (Small Catechism).

Perhaps one person's needs aren't quite the same as another's, since we differ from each other. That doesn't matter. Whatever we need, God wants us to tell him about it.

Notice the word "daily." That means "each day." And here it means that we can ask God for whatever we need, but we shouldn't ask for more than we need each day.

Don't ask for things you may need tomorrow. Wait until tomorrow comes, and then ask God for whatever you need that day.

God doesn't want you to worry about anything, and he knows that one day is all we can handle at a time. God will take care of your tomorrow, and the next day, and the next day, and forever.

Give us this day our daily bread ℞ ℞ ℞

When the children of Israel were wandering in the wilderness, God provided them with food. Yet they were told to gather up enough manna to last a day, and no more. They were not to put anything away for tomorrow.

And when Jesus spoke from the mount, he told us to "take therefore no thought for the morrow . . . " (Matthew 6:34).

Now here, in this prayer, we are asking for *daily* bread—not enough to last a week, a year, or a lifetime— only enough for this day.

There is a reason for this emphasis on the present. We cannot see into the future, but God can. Only he knows what we will need tomorrow or the next day, or for the rest of our lives. And he will provide it. But he wants us to realize that. He wants us

to understand that we are dependent upon him. In fact, he wants to remind us daily. And so we are to pray only for what we need today, knowing that God will be there to take care of tomorrow—and all the tomorrows to come.

In other words, let's live one day at a time—which is very sound advice.

Jesus tells us to ask for *our* daily bread," not "my daily bread"—which means that we ourselves must be part of the answer to this prayer. For we are asking God to help us share what we have with those who have not.

At the present time, there is enough food, enough water, enough clothing, and there could be enough shelter for everyone's basic needs to be met. But some of us have more than we need and others not enough. The real problem is in distribution, in bringing together the need and the resource.

Our daily bread is a gift that, once received by us, is to be given again.

And, as in the miracle of the loaves and fishes, once we are willing to let others share what we have—and as we manage life and its resources responsibly and sensitively—there will be enough for all. But there is never enough until we give it away.

We ask God to give us "our" daily bread because when we pray we are thinking of our brothers and sisters all over the world. Some don't have as much as we have. Some need much more than we need.

So when we ask God for something, let's think about how we can share what he gives us with someone who needs it. Maybe we can try not to waste our food by not taking more on our plates than we can eat. Then we won't have to throw any food away. And the money we save on our family food can go to the church hunger fund—or to other people in our city or town who care for the hungry and the poor. Maybe we can remember not to keep the water running, so that people who need water can have more.

Maybe you can think of lots of other ways to share the good things God gives you. When you pray, ask God to give you more ideas.

And forgive us our debts

A debt is something we owe to God or to another person.

Remember when we talked about doing God's will? Well, doing his will is something we owe to God. And when we do what we want to do instead of what God wants us to do, then we aren't giving God what belongs to him. We know we have done something wrong or haven't done something right, and we feel uncomfortable about it. We feel as if God isn't close to us anymore. He wants to be, but we won't let him because we know we have been wrong and we feel bad. And sometimes we even wonder how he could still love us. But God *does* love us, even when we do wrong things! He forgives us, which means that we feel very close to him again.

Just ask him, and you'll see. If you've done something wrong and are sorry—truly!—just ask God to forgive you and believe that he has. Jesus promised. Then you'll feel that nothing stands between you and God any longer. Go ahead. Ask him.

One of the worst feelings we can have is to do something wrong and know it. We seem to be out of kilter with the rest of the world, and, what is more uncomfortable, we feel cut off from God.

Certain things belong to God, and when we don't fulfill our obligations to him, we go into debt. When we insist on following our will instead of God's will, we close the door of our hearts in his face. The wonderful closeness that comes from living a life that honors his name is gone. We feel separated because we *are* separated. In fact, sin means separation—the separation that comes to us when God goes one way and we choose to go another. We get just plain lost!

That is why forgiveness is so necessary. It's not a formality of "I'm sorry" and "Well, you ought to be!" Forgiveness is getting back in touch with God, readmitting him to our hearts, where he belongs and wants to be. It isn't difficult. We don't have to beg or grovel or do anything other than want forgiveness and ask God for it. You see, he has already forgiven us. Through Christ, his Son, he has already paid the penalty for the wrongs we have done or the rights we have not done. His love can heal the hurts we do to each other and take away the terrible guilt that cripples us.

Do you miss God when you do something wrong? Well, God misses that closeness with you, too. And he's waiting to hear you say, "Lord, forgive me."

as we forgive our debtors 🙢 🙢

But now you have to do the same thing for others that God did for you.

Is there someone who hurt you? Are you angry with somebody who did something you didn't like? Did someone take something from you and won't give it back? Then somebody owes you something. Somebody is in debt to you—and that makes the person a debtor.

What you have to do is forgive that person. And the reason you have to do it is because God forgives you when you do something wrong. It isn't fair to let God forgive you and then not forgive someone else. And God is very fair. That's why he can forgive you only as you forgive others.

But forgiveness is a two-way street. God can forgive us *only* as we forgive those who hurt us. God isn't being stubborn—but he knows that as long as our hearts are knotted up tight as a fist against anybody, they aren't open to receive what *he* offers, either.

Maybe the hurt we feel is too big for us to handle. Maybe we just *can't* love the person who inflicted it. And we don't want to be hypocrites and say we forgive someone when deep down inside we know it isn't so. That's all right. What we can't do, God can. There isn't any hurt too big for him to forgive. There isn't any person he can't love. And he understands how we feel. But he wants us to give him our hurt and our resentment. He wants to heal us, to drain the hurt from us. He wants us to ask him to help us forgive by giving us the greateartedness and compassion that are in him. He wants us to ask him to make us more loving than we could ever be by ourselves. And if we ask, our tightly knotted hearts will open—to him, to others, and to the gift of forgiveness itself.

✍ And lead us not into temptation

Sometimes we want to do something we know we shouldn't do. That's a temptation.

And the best thing to do when that happens is to say "No!" to ourselves, because we know that God wouldn't want us to do something wrong.

Sometimes it isn't easy to say No. But it's good to learn how to say it, because lots of times we will have to say No—especially if we want to keep on doing the things God wants us to do.

It's easier to say No if you let God help you.

Would God, who loves us so much, actually lead us into temptation? If not, then why are we asking him not to?

The Greek word used in the original means either "trial" or "test," as one would test something for its strength and endurance—and perhaps that is easier for us to understand. The New English Bible translates it: "Do not bring us to the test." Temptation implies evil, and we're no match for that. But tests and trials are the hard times of life, and while we don't look forward to them, they can do a lot for us. "Count it all joy," James says, "when you meet various trials, for you know that the testing of your faith produces steadfastness" (James 1:2). It is important for us to know that God wills us good. But, in the words of Leslie Weatherhead, "What is not his will can be his instrument."

So what we are really doing here is asking God to be with us in the hard times, and not to make them any harder than we can handle. Everyone needs to be tested, to find out where his strengths and weaknesses lie. We just don't want to be tested to the breaking point. And God promises us we won't be. "No temptation has overtaken you that is not common to man. God is faithful, and he will not let you be tempted beyond your strength, but with the temptation will also provide the way of escape, that you may be able to endure it" (I Corinthians 10:13).

Yes, we will be tempted, and yes, we will be tried, but we will not be crushed. Elsewhere Paul says we may "be knocked down—but never knocked out" (II Corinthians 6:9). We are stronger than we think, because we aren't alone.

but deliver us from evil ⚡ ⚡

Evil is a very ugly thing, and there is a lot of evil in the world. When people lie and steal and hurt and hate and kill and think bad things about each other, that is evil.

You don't want to do anything evil, and I don't, either. But sometimes we do things that are very, very wrong, and it seems we just can't help ourselves. That's because evil is stronger than we are—and because then we're not trusting God to be our helper. Because the only one who is stronger than evil is God.

So when you feel that you are going to do something evil, stop and talk to God right away. God is always ready to keep you away from anything evil. And he can do it, because he is the most powerful force in all the world.

We may debate it, but the Bible makes no bones about it—there is a power of evil in this world. The proper translation of this word is "the evil one" (the New English Bible says, "Save us from the evil one"), none other than Satan, the Accuser, the Prince of Darkness. He is no figment of the imagination. He is very real and he is at war with God. In the words of Karl Barth, "Satan is the one who always says 'no' to God!" His aim is to win us over to his side, because that is the way he can cause God the greatest amount of pain.

Watch out for this evil one. He knows where we are vulnerable. He knows we become overconfident about our strengths. He loves to play on our doubts and fears. He is much, much more powerful than we are, so don't try to fight him alone. You can't win. Only God can, because only God is stronger. And we have God's promise that he will deliver us from this evil one—if we will accept his strength: "He has delivered us from the dominion of darkness and transferred us to the dominion of his beloved Son" (Colossians 1:13). God has disarmed Satan, and the only power he has over us now is the power we give him when we disbelieve God.

In this final petition, we are asking our Father to protect us from all that is evil. Knowing we have this deliverance, we can face the unknowns of the future without fear.

For thine is the kingdom, and the power, and the glory . . . forever ⁊ ⁊

We are near the end of our prayer now, and we want to tell God how great he is.

Think about all the things we have learned about prayer. . . . Think about everything God does for us and in us.

Now—tell God how much you love him!

Most scholars agree that this phrase was added on to the Lord's Prayer and probably comes from the Jewish custom of ending a prayer by praising God. But it is in keeping with everything Jesus taught us, because it says, quite simply, that God is everything, and everything is his, and it will be that way forever.

Praise comes naturally at this point. We are not the same as we were when we began to pray. We have touched God, and we have opened our lives to him—not only for the moments it took us to pray, but for all time. How can we help but rise up in confidence, blessing God for his magnificence, his power, his glory, and—wonder of wonders!—his love for us!

Amen 𝒵 𝒵

"Amen" means "Yes, this is the way it is," "So be it," and we often find it at the end of a prayer.

And we say "Amen" here because—yes, we mean it.

You won't find a big explanation for "amen" anywhere. In Greek the word means "verily" or "truly, truly," and at the end of a prayer it means "So be it." In other words, in a conversation it was used as a spiritual form of italics or an exclamation point to mark something very important. And in our worship today, we use it to say, "Hear! Hear! That goes for me, too!"

Most of the times Jesus used "amen," he was speaking to his disciples, as if to say, "Now, listen carefully. . . ." That seems to be what he is saying to us about everything he has taught us in the Lord's Prayer.

"Amen," then, means not the end of a conversation with God, but the beginning of a life wonderfully centered around him. Truly, truly.

THE LORD'S PRAYER

Our Father who art in heaven, ⚡ ⚡ ⚡ ⚡
Hallowed be thy name. Thy kingdom come.
Thy will be done on earth, as it is in heaven.
Give us this day our daily bread. ⚡ ⚡ ⚡
And forgive us our debts, ⚡ ⚡ ⚡ ⚡ ⚡
⚡ ⚡ ⚡ ⚡ ⚡ as we forgive our debtors.
And lead us not into temptation, ⚡ ⚡ ⚡
⚡ ⚡ ⚡ ⚡ ⚡ ⚡ but deliver us from evil:
For thine is the kingdom, and the power, ⚡
and the glory . . . forever. Amen. ⚡ ⚡ ⚡

MATTHEW 6: 9b-13